# Picture the Past
# Life in AMERICA'S FIRST CITIES

Sally Senzell Isaacs

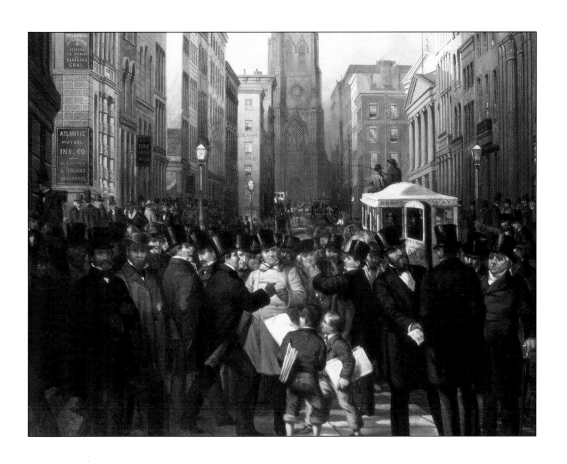

Heinemann Library
Chicago, Illinois

© 2000 Reed Educational & Professional Publishing
Published by Heinemann Library,
an imprint of Reed Educational & Professional Publishing,
Chicago, IL

Customer Service 888-454-2279

Visit our website at www.heinemannlibrary.com

Produced for Heinemann Library by Bender Richardson
White.
Editor: Lionel Bender
Designer: Ben White
Picture Researcher: Cathy Stastny
Media Conversion and Typesetting: MW Graphics
Production Controller: Kim Richardson

09 08
10 9 8 7 6 5 4

Printed in China

Library of Congress Cataloging-in-Publication Data.
Isaacs, Sally Senzell, 1950–
    Life in Americas First Cities/Sally Senzell Isaacs.
        p. cm.  (Picture the past)
    Includes bibliographical references and index.
    Summary: Introduces the daily lives of people who
settled in the first cities in the United States, discussing
houses, clothing, schools and work.

ISBN 1-57572-315-8 (lib. bdg.)  1-58810-299-8 (pbk.)
1. United States-Social life and customs-1783-1865-
Juvenile literature. 2. City and town life-United States-
History-19th century-Juvenile literature. 3. Cities and
towns--United States-History-19th century-Juvenile
literature. (1. City and town life-History 19th century. 2.
Citied and towns-History-19th century. 3. United States-
Social life and customs-1783-1865.) I. Title.

E164 .I83 2000
973'0973'2-dc21                          99-089882

Special thanks to Mike Carpenter, Scott Westerfield, and
Tristan Boyer-Binns at Heinemann Library for editorial and
design guidance and direction.

**Acknowledgments**
The producers and publishers are grateful to the
following for permission to reproduce copyright material:

The Bridgman Art Library; Library of Congress,
Washington D.C., 9; Museum of the City of New York, pp.
1, 3, 10, 17, 26; New York Historical Society, p. 25; Corbis:
Corbis, pp. 27, 30; Minnesota Historical Society, p. 24;
Hulton Getty/Jacob A. Riis, p. 19; Peter Newark's
American Pictures, pp. 8, 13, 15, 18, 22, 23;
Consultants/Smithsonian Institute, p. 21.

Cover photograph: Peter Newark's American Pictures.

Illustrations by John James, p. 20; Gerald Wood, p. 14;
James Field, pp. 12, 30; Nick Heweston, p. 7.
Maps by Stefan Chabluk.
Cover make-up by Mike Pilley, Pelican Graphics.

**Note the the Reader**
Some words are shown in bold, **like this**.
You can find out what they mean by looking in the
glossary.

## ABOUT THIS BOOK

This book tells about daily life in cities in the United States in the years 1800 to 1860. At this time, most Americans did not live in cities. They lived on farms. But cities were growing quickly. People looking for jobs moved to America's cities. They moved from farms. They moved from other countries, too.
We have illustrated the book with paintings and drawings from this time and with artists' ideas of how things looked then. In the 1850s, photography started to become popular, and we have included historic photographs from some of the first U.S. cities.

### The Consultant

Special thanks go to Diane Smolinski for her help in the preparation of this series. Diane Smolinski has years of experience interpreting standards documents and putting them into practice.

### The Author

Sally Senzell Isaacs is a professional writer and editor of nonfiction books for children. She graduated from Indiana University, earning a B.S. degree in Education with majors in American History and Sociology. For some years, she was the Editorial Director of Reader's Digest Educational Division. Sally Senzell Isaacs lives in New Jersey with her husband and two children.

# CONTENTS

# Towns Become Cities

Starting around 1800, many farmers moved to towns to escape the long hours, hard outdoor work, and loneliness of farming. They took jobs in factories, stores, and offices. Tens of thousands of people from Europe moved to new American towns to escape wars, lack of food, and poverty in their homelands. They hoped to earn money and give their children a better life. Slowly the towns grew into cities. By 1860, cities such as Boston and New York had more than 500,000 people.

**LOOK FOR THESE**
The illustration of a city boy and girl sits alongside the title of each double-page story in the book.

The picture of an apartment building marks boxes with interesting facts about city life.

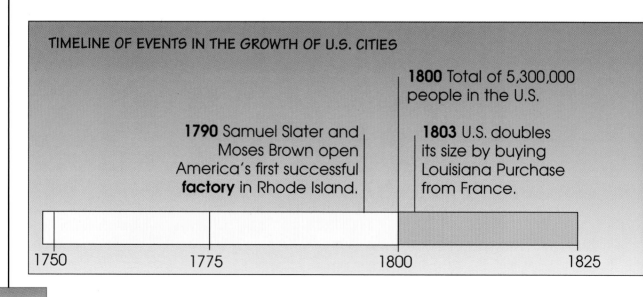

**TIMELINE OF EVENTS IN THE GROWTH OF U.S. CITIES**

**1800** Total of 5,300,000 people in the U.S.

**1790** Samuel Slater and Moses Brown open America's first successful **factory** in Rhode Island.

**1803** U.S. doubles its size by buying Louisiana Purchase from France.

| 1750 | 1775 | 1800 | 1825 |

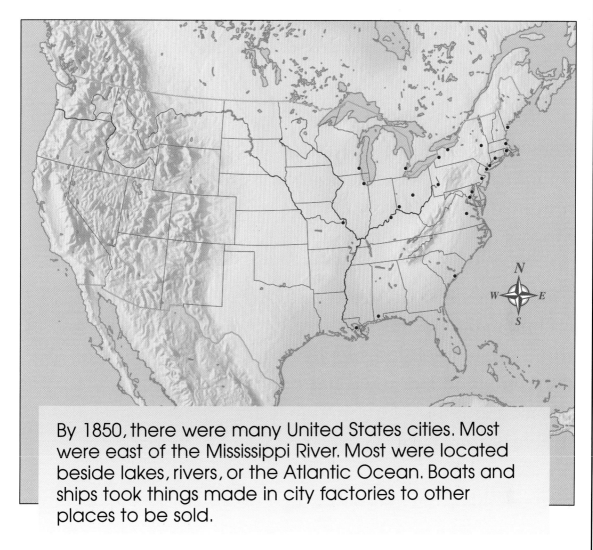

By 1850, there were many United States cities. Most were east of the Mississippi River. Most were located beside lakes, rivers, or the Atlantic Ocean. Boats and ships took things made in city factories to other places to be sold.

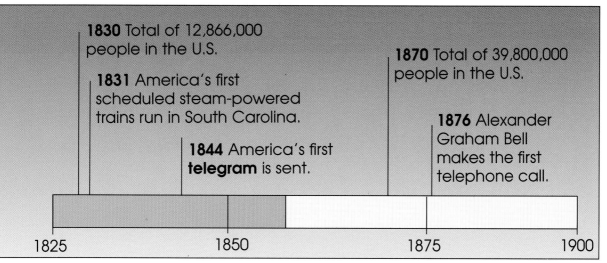

**1830** Total of 12,866,000 people in the U.S.

**1831** America's first scheduled steam-powered trains run in South Carolina.

**1844** America's first **telegram** is sent.

**1870** Total of 39,800,000 people in the U.S.

**1876** Alexander Graham Bell makes the first telephone call.

1825          1850          1875          1900

# Busy Streets

A city was an exciting place. There were stores around every corner with things for sale. There were libraries, restaurants, theaters, and museums. Most of all, there were jobs.

Cities sometimes grew too fast. More and more people moved there. Stores could not get enough supplies for everyone. Builders could not build streets and houses fast enough. City streets became crowded with people, horses, and **carriages**. There were no traffic lights to help control the flow.

Large stores, like this one in Boston around 1850, sold everything needed for the home. Here, people shop for tablecloths, curtains, and material for clothes.

## DIRTY STREET

Cities could be smelly places. People threw garbage out the front door. Then they let their pet pigs run free to eat the garbage.

This part of New York City had fancy stores and rich people. Poor people lived and shopped in another part of the city.

# Getting News

There were no TVs, radios, movie theaters, or telephones. There were only newspapers. People heard most of their news from a neighbor—who heard it from a friend—who heard it from a traveler at the hotel.

City post offices displayed notices and kept copies of newspapers for everyone to read. News from towns far away often took several days to reach the city.

People mailed letters to one another. If a message had to reach someone quickly, a person went to the post office or **telegraph** office to send a **telegram**. The person told the message to a worker. The worker put the message in code and sent it through telegraph wires. A worker in another city read the code and wrote down the message.

Steam-driven printing presses, the electric telegraph, steamboats, and steam locomotives allowed news to travel fast and cities to grow.

# Transportation

Cities were not very large. It took about thirty minutes to walk from one end of a city to the other. Still, Americans always liked to find faster ways to move. Some city people rode an **omnibus**. They sat on wooden benches and bounced along the bumpy streets.

Omnibuses and **carriages** move along Broadway, a busy street in New York City. An omnibus usually carried twelve people at a time.

Small boats carried goods and people to city harbors from towns upriver or along the coast.

Many people rode **stagecoaches** from one city to another. A trip could take three days, riding eighteen hours a day. It was sometimes easier to travel by boat. Boats were also better for sending loads of **factory**-made goods.

# Homes and Houses

Cities had many **apartment** buildings. Poor families squeezed together into a small apartment. The rooms were cold in the winter and hot in the summer. Children shared the bedroom with their parents. Many families shared a bathroom in the hall.

In this cutaway of an apartment building, the row of rooms on the left belongs to one family. It shows the:
1. living room
2. kitchen
3. bedroom
4. bathroom
5. neighbor's apartment
6. chimneys

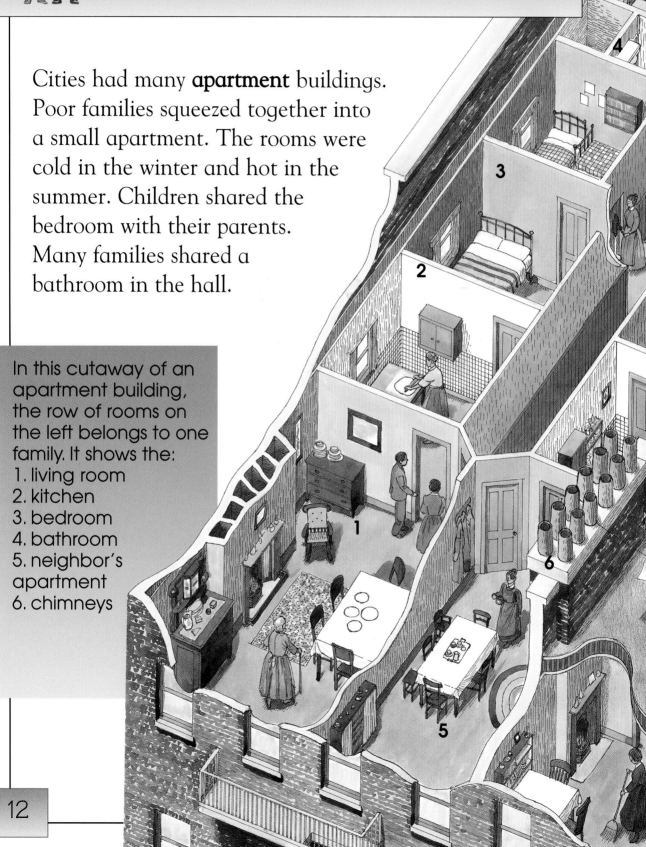

Some people lived in larger houses. There, children had their own bedrooms. The family ate together in the kitchen. For special times, they ate in a dining room. In 1850, not even the richest people had electric lights. They were not invented yet.

## BATH TIME
To have a bath, people dragged a round tub into the kitchen or bathroom. They filled the tub with boiling water. They had a bath once a week.

Having one's own room for sleeping and playing was a luxury.
In 1850, houses did NOT have:
• air conditioning
• refrigerators
• televisions
• built-in bath tubs

# Adults at Work

There were many kinds of jobs in the city. Some people worked in stores and offices. Some worked in schools and churches. Many men and women worked in **factories**. They stood by big machines twelve hours a day, six days a week.

This cutaway of a cotton **mill** shows:
1. men unloading raw cotton
2. and 3. women working spinning and weaving machines
4. men repairing machines

Factories made many things, such as clothes, shoes, guns, and clocks. They used machines powered by steam or running water. Each worker did one small job all day. In a skirt factory, one worker checked the thread. Another sewed the buttons. The jobs were boring and did not pay much.

## FAST MACHINES

In earlier times, a shoemaker could make two to three pairs of shoes a day. A factory machine could make hundreds of shoes a day.

The first factories were noisy and dangerous. There was little fresh air.

15

# Children at Work

Many city children had no time to go to school. They ran off to the **factory** each morning and worked there all day. They earned about two dollars a week. Their families needed this money to help pay for food and **rent**.

WORK DAY

5:00 A.M.: Wake up
6:00 A.M.: Start working
Noon : Quick break for lunch
6:00 P.M.: Go home to eat
8:00 P.M.: Go to sleep

Children did jobs needing tiny fingers. Often they had accidents with the machines.

Factory owners liked to **hire** children. They paid children less money than adults. Children could fit behind the machines to fix threads. They could sweep under the machines, too.

City children also worked in houses and on the streets. Some of them worked as **servants** for rich people.

Children sold newspapers and matches on the streets. They also delivered goods and cleaned chimneys.

# School

Today, all children must go to school. Most schools are free. Before 1850, not every child went to school. Many children worked. Parents had to pay for school, except for very poor families. Free African-Americans living in the North were not allowed in the same schools with white children.

A school had only one room. Sometimes 100 students of all ages sat together.

The school day usually started with prayers and saluting the U.S. flag.

The classroom was usually very plain. In most schools, there were no maps or posters on the wall. Students sat on benches with writing tables in front of them. Children practiced writing words for many hours.

## BOSTON SCHOOLS

Around 1850, Boston schools tried a new idea. Students of the same age sat together in the same classroom. Every student sat at a desk!

# School Lessons

Boys and girls usually went to school together. Some schools were for girls only. Some were for boys only.

## WRITING LESSONS

In most schools, children wrote on slates using slate pencils or sticks of white chalk.

To practice her school work at home, a young girl sewed these letters and numbers into a piece of cloth. She used a needle and lengths of colored threads.

## WRITING PAPER

Some teachers made writing notebooks for the class. They folded paper and stitched it. Then they drew the writing lines.

In the classroom, some children wrote while others read out loud or practiced math problems. Children helped take care of the school. In winter, older children arrived early to start a fire and sweep the floor.

All children learned math, reading, writing, spelling, and history. They also learned good manners. In some schools, children had to stand in front of the teacher and spell their spelling words. Before speaking, children bowed to the teacher.

# Clothes for Adults

Before the 1800s, men wore short pants, bunched at the knee. In the 1800s, long pants became the new style. Men still wore knee pants for sports, such as running and shooting.

Outdoors, most men and women usually wore hats.

Women would never think of wearing pants. They also thought it was wrong to show their ankles! They wore long dresses to go shopping and to go to fancy parties. They wore long dresses to work in **factories**. They even wore long dresses for swimming. Women wanted their waists to look tiny. They laced them up in **corsets**.

Women wore a **petticoat** and hoops made of steel wire and webbing under a dress to puff it out.

# Clothes for Children

Some children had very fancy clothes. Boys wore vests and jackets trimmed with soft velvet. Girls wore **petticoats** under their dresses. They also wore long, lacy pants under their dresses. The pants were called drawers.

Children might wear these clothes to a birthday party or to go shopping in the city.

# WINTER CLOTHES

Warm winter boots cost a lot of money. Poor parents stuffed straw and newspaper inside shoes to keep their children's feet warm.

Some families had no money to buy fancy clothes. A boy might wear the same pants and shirt year after year. A girl might wear the same dress. She always wore an apron over the dress to keep it as clean as possible.

In winter, rich parents bought their children thick coats and mittens or a muff to keep their hands warm.

# Getting Food

People stored food for a short time in an ice box. This was a wooden chest with a block of ice inside. They bought ice on the street from a traveling salesman.

City homes had no room for gardens. People could not grow their own vegetables. They could not raise animals for meat. Trains and carts brought food from the farms to markets in the city.

## BOTTLED FOODS

Some people put raw fish and vegetables in glass jars filled with **vinegar**. Others put cooked fruits and vegetables in glass jars. This kept these foods from **spoiling**.

There were no refrigerators in these days. People mostly used food that did not spoil, such as potatoes, onions, flour, and cornmeal. If they bought a turkey or fish, they cooked it right away. Raw eggs were too difficult to transport without being broken.

## HOME DELIVERY

Many cities did not allow people to own cows. Farmers delivered milk and butter to city homes every day.

In this busy city neighborhood, people bought food every day from carts in the street.

# A Simple Meal

At most houses, meals were very simple. There were few fresh fruits and vegetables. Many meals were just bread and potatoes.

Everyone in a family ate together. Meals were served and eaten in the living room. After the meal, plates, pots, and pans were washed by hand.

At Thanksgiving and other holidays, relatives might be invited for a meal. Everyone would help in the kitchen.

# City Recipe—Potato Soup

Follow the instructions below to make potato soup as city people did in the early 1800s. Potato soup was an easy and cheap meal to make. This recipe makes enough hot potato soup for six helpings.

WARNING: Do not cook anything unless there is an adult to help you. Always ask an adult to do the cutting and cooking on a hot stove.

**YOU WILL NEED**
2 white potatoes, peeled and cut into small cubes
1 medium-size onion, cut in small pieces
2 tablespoons of butter
2 cups (480 ml) milk
2 teaspoons flour
1 teaspoon salt
dash of pepper

**FOLLOW THE STEPS**

1. Place the potatoes and onions in a pot and cover with water.
2. Cook until the potatoes are soft.
3. Pour the mixture in a strainer and drain off the water. Save the potatoes and onions.

4. Melt the butter in a pan.
5. Stir in the flour and cook gently for one minute.
6. Remove the pan from the heat and stir in the milk, salt, and pepper.

7. Put the pan back on the heat and stir until the milk boils.
8. Stir in the potato and onion mixture. Heat for two more minutes.
9. Serve hot in bowls, with bread.

# How Cities Changed

From around 1850, America's cities grew bigger very quickly. More people moved to cities from farms and from other countries. By 1860, cities were **hiring** garbage collectors, police, and fire fighters to make the streets safer and healthier. **Factories** became safer, too. Young children were no longer allowed to work in factories and **mills**. Instead, they all went to school.

BIGGEST U.S. CITY

In 1800, there were 60,000 people living in New York City. By 1900, there were two million people living in the city.

This photo shows a street scene in New York City, 1865.

# Glossary

**apartment** one of many rooms or sets of rooms within a building in which people live. In cities, run-down apartment buildings are known as tenements.

**carriage** type of transportation pulled by horses that was used to carry people and goods

**corset** clothing worn by women under a dress to squeeze the waist and make it look smaller

**factory** building where things are made in large numbers or amounts, usually with the help of machines

**hire** to take on and pay someone to do a job

**mill** factory where products, such as cloth, paper, glass, furniture, and steel, are made

**omnibus** wooden car pulled by horses that had several seats for passengers to travel round towns and cities

**petticoat** thin, lightweight skirt worn under a skirt or dress

**rent** money paid to live or work in someone else's building or house

**servant** someone who works in another person's house, usually cooking, cleaning, and serving

**spoil** to become rotten

**stagecoach** boxlike car pulled by horses in which people traveled long distances

**telegram** message sent by telegraph

**telegraph** machine that sends messages over wires in the form of a code

**vinegar** sour liquid usually made from wines

# More Books to Read

An older reader can help you with these books:

Thompson, Ware. *Cities: The Building of America*. Danbury, Conn.: Children's Press, 1997.

Toynton, Evelyn. *Growing up in America: 1830-1860*. Brookfield, Conn.: Millbrook Press, Incorporated, 1995.

# Index